Exploring
the Fruits of the Spirit with Joy

Love, Joy, & Peace

By Diana Robinson

www.transformedpublishing.com

This book belongs to

_____.

Gifted with love,

by _____.

And the Lord spoke to Moses, saying: "Speak to Aaron and his sons, saying, 'This is the way you shall bless the children of Israel. Say to them: "The Lord bless you and keep you; The Lord make His face shine upon you, And be gracious to you; The Lord lift up His countenance upon you, And give you peace."'
"So they shall put My name on the children of Israel, and
I will bless them."
Numbers 6:22-27

PEACE
is the **POWER**
to be full of **JOY** and
LOVE
even when things
DO NOT GO MY WAY

Galatians 5:22-23
But the fruit of the Spirit is love, joy, peace, longsuffering, kindness, goodness, faithfulness, gentleness, self-control. Against such there is no law.

Sometimes my block tower begins to sway. Because I have Jesus' PEACE, I will be okay. I choose to be full of joy and love, even when things do not go my way.

Sometimes my sandcastle gets washed away. Because I have Jesus' PEACE, I will be okay. I choose to be full of joy and love, even when things do not go my way.

Sometimes when it is time to leave, I still want to stay. Because I have Jesus' PEACE, I will be okay. I choose to be full of joy and love, even when things do not go my way.

Sometimes people have mean things to say. Because I have Jesus' **PEACE**, I will be okay. I choose to be **full** of joy and love, even when things do not go my way.

Sometimes I want to buy something and my parents say, "NO WAY!" Because I have Jesus' PEACE, I will be okay. I choose to be full of joy and love, even when things do not go my way.

Sometimes I'm not ready
to go to bed at the
end of the day.
Because I have Jesus'
PEACE, I will be okay.
I choose to be full of joy
and love, even when things
do not go my way.

Jesus said, "Peace I leave with you, My peace I give to you; not as the world gives do I give to you. Let not your heart be troubled, neither let it be afraid.

John 14:27

Who is Jesus?

Jesus is the Son of God, who was sent to live on the earth. Jesus teaches us how to build and live in the Kingdom of God while we are on the earth. He also teaches us to anticipate the glorious Kingdom of Heaven, which is every believer's eternal home.

Because of Jesus' great love for us, He paid our sin debt in full with His precious blood on the cross. All of us who believe and accept His gift, enter into right standing with God and are heirs of His Kingdom.

You are LOVED. You were created for great purpose. You are forgiven of all wrongdoing. Ask God for help and guidance each day. Know the Holy Spirit lives in you and will comfort, teach, and empower you.

In Jesus Name,
Amen

Also by Diana Robinson

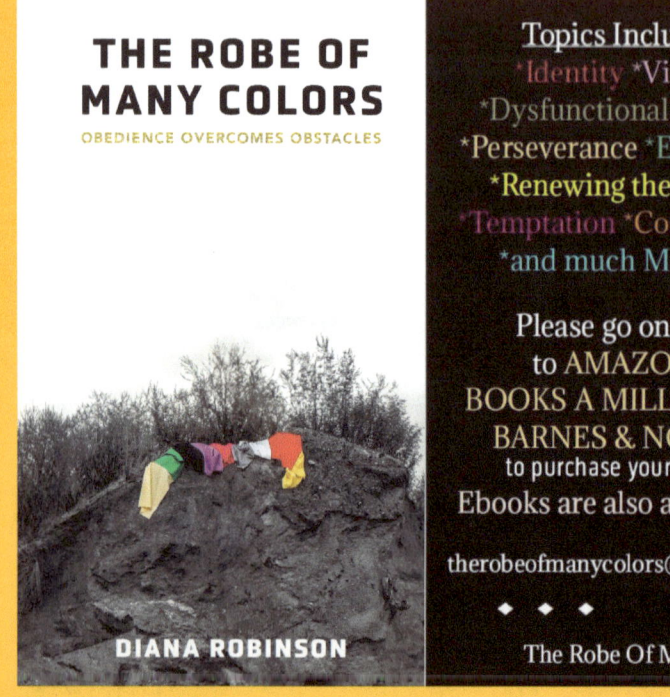

The Robe of Many Colors is a resource to combat anxiety, disappointment, discouragement, temptation, distraction, inferiority, and oppression.

Despite what the circumstances look like, and the intensity of the fiery darts raging to root in your mind - *you are well able to overcome all!*

This book is for people searching for answers to common questions, such as:

- What about me?
- When will things turn around for me?
- Why me?

The Robe of Many Colors will awaken the *vision* within you to operate confidently in all God has entrusted and equipped you with. This book is loaded with practical and relevant Bible-base teaching! Proven principles from the life of Joseph are the framework for each chapter. Discover the benefits of obedience.

Exploring
the Fruits of the Spirit with Joy

Longsuffering, Kindness, & Goodness

Learning to climb a rock wall is hard at first. Even when my mood wants to be at its worst, I choose to be kind and do good. I say thank you to the people who help me and do my best every time. Because of longsuffering, I completed a goal of mine!

Exploring the Fruits of the Spirit with Joy
Love, Joy, & Peace

By Diana Robinson
© Copyright 2020 by Diana Robinson
All rights reserved
ISBN-13: 9781953241009
Published by Transformed Publishing
Contributing Author Joanna Pettis
Photography Courtesy of MR-AH Photography
www.mrahphotography.com

All rights reserved solely by the author. No part of this book may be reproduced, stored in a retrieval system, or transmitted in any form or by any means without expressed written permission of the author.

Scripture taken from the New King James Version®. Copyright © 1982 by Thomas Nelson. Used by permission. All rights reserved.

Do you have an idea for a book featuring your child?

Please contact us today!

Website: www.transformedpublishing.com
Email: transformedpublishing@gmail.com

www.ingramcontent.com/pod-product-compliance
Lightning Source LLC
Chambersburg PA
CBHW041217070526
44583CB00001B/18